A GREEN LIGHT

MATTHEW ROHRER

A GREEN LIGHT

VERSE PRESS *Amherst, Massachusetts*

Published by Verse Press

Copyright © 2004 by Verse Press
Library of Congress Cataloging-in-Publication Data
Rohrer, Matthew.
  A green light / Matthew Rohrer. — 1st ed.
    p. cm.
  ISBN 0-9723487-7-8 (pbk. : alk. paper)
  I. Title.
  PS3568.052 G74 2004
  811'.54—dc22   2003019292

9 8 7 6 5 4 3 2 1

FIRST EDITION

CONTENTS

This book was written for Susan

A GREEN LIGHT

MY SOUP

The soup pond is bright green
brilliant, amazing, starlight green
and still as a lawn. It isn't
filthy, it's full of flowers,
though people think it's filthy.
A fat man walks backwards
slapping his ass with a whip.
This is not filthy.
A hawk or something
lolligags overhead, a lazy line
in the blue, and a powerful male voice
of unclear origin tells you so.
Who is this, who is speaking to you?
Are the armies of bugs that fly
through your memory his legions?
His lies fly forwards and backwards
in time. You are not safe here,
they are coming this way.

I HAIL FROM THE BOTTOM OF THE SEA, THE LAND OF ETERNAL DARKNESS

I go out among my countrymen:
the fat man who works beside me
in a sphere of his own foulness:
the man born with no nose
who's turned to Satan: I stand
at the window of the office building and look
out over the starlit harbor: to the women
no one looks at: I look at them:
to tear out my eyebrows in anguish:
no one watches over us unless our uncles
are flying planes: we take up defensive positions
against the machinations of the universe: we don't
even know what we are: we take up arms against God:
then quickly take defensive measures: someone
threw a frog at me: I walk out in the bright air
among my countrymen: I have been all around
the world and I know everyone is lying

THE ADORABLE LITTLE BOY

Today my ski boots disintegrated on my feet.
It is getting more difficult to play
the role of The Adorable Little Boy
now, and I will confirm what most of you
have suspected: I am ill,
I have the distinct sensation that my head
is donut-shaped. But don't let that
stop me from wriggling my way
into your hearts, those of you
who are not empty blue suits.
I am still very aware, I am hyper-aware.
A beautiful ass makes me sneeze and cough!
But now I suspect you are looking for something
and here it is: Pliny described trees that speak.

DISQUISITION ON TREES

The book that says the President is a friend of trees is a book of lies! The President should read the one about the little mouse that drove a car and got his girlfriend pregnant and they had to fly a rubberband-powered airplane over a stack of newspapers. Not a tree in sight. Not a tree in the whole book. Another book that he might pick up casually could strip the veil of illusion from his eyes: pretty women, the unpleasant foot odors of. But that is only what it appears to be about. It is a book about how to have a big piece missing from your head and live.

C

Imagine a place that never sees
feelings of calm moving into me.

Shadows soften the stones
and a great deal of rhetoric

is unstoppable. Bird music peppers
all the thin trees.

I'm going to imagine a staircase
for emptiness, and a little hole

until I feel my soul.
This is the built-in contradiction

of a tree, a thin unlikely place
outside a fancy restaurant.

MK ULTRA

Now turn your attentions
to the dreamers moving
through the snowdrifts,
their musical instruments
are zoomorphic,
and the appearance of white,
angelic women pushing
baby carriages
is a sign from Heaven.
I'm in bed and my stomach aches
because I ate too much.
If the question is:
what has replaced
God in my life,
the gene that determines that
is probably not
going to be selected for.

Precious needles,
I could swallow them
when they show us films
about handicapped kids
making it in our world.
She says, White culture
has a long history of enslaving,
raping, segregating
and discriminating:
does that mean she's thinking of me?
Just waiting for a chance
to disguise her fear
as I downshift into a particular neighborhood?
I will not last long in the forest
where the picnic went wrong.

He said "the conservation of matter
is a Christian ideal,
and they have special lights
which prevent us from dancing.
If you only had a machine
you could find out for yourself."

But what good is an incantation
against an Empire?
The answer is on the side
of the moon we're not supposed to see.
How painful to walk through town
in a dented suit of armor,
early summer, the whole neighborhood
smells like sperm,
and it's late,
scars of oral surgery.

Past the incredible rock
where the picnic went wrong
the trees were half-red,
with reluctance.
A line of bright machines
is silent in the sky.
Have you ever felt
that the answers to all your questions
lie somewhere UP THERE?
Now turn your attentions
to the dreamer moving
through the snowdrifts.
I pick a flower for you every day
and keep it with my ammunition.
I fear that I am becoming an insane pervert.
Can you predict what kind
of balding fat man
I'll be? Your eyes are so treacherous
I'm going to bury them.

In the center of the universe
is an enormous emptiness
that's teaching us something
about ourselves.
Early summer,
the whole neighborhood smells
like sperm. The birds just sound pitiful.
The appearance of white,
angelic women
pushing baby carriages
is a sign from Heaven
and if you only had a machine
you could find it for yourself.

And now I'm in bed
and my stomach aches
because I ate too much.
We had one for the road
and it was late.

They are afraid
to admit there is beauty
and quality in this world,
because somewhere
each morning,
someone wakes up
and they're suffering terribly!

I'm going to sit here until I feel my soul.

———

[I felt, at this point, that my brain was easing apart and two distinct but simultaneous consciousnesses were developing]

But at the end of dinner
the candelabra excused itself into the night.

The patron saint of corridors
and hallways said
the conservation of matter
is just a Christian ideal.
The next day he ate the most
gorgonzola he'd ever eaten.
The gene that determines this
is probably not
going to be selected for,
and a burst of trumpets over the park
announces the return of precious needles.
How painful to walk around
on the side of the moon
we're not allowed to see.

Recently I've been dreaming
of cursing old people
with little provocation,
because their culture
has a long history of enslaving,
raping, and segregating,
and they have special lights
which prevent us from dancing.

Drinking and being exceptionally
social and not working
and drinking before getting together
shows a "lack of respect."

And they were disturbed,
I suppose, to find out
I had been transporting
psychedelic mushrooms.
What do animals think?
They think I will not last long in the forest.

He was afraid to admit
there was beauty
and quality in this world.
But at the end of dinner
the candelabra excused itself into the night.
The next day he ate
the most gorgonzola
he'd ever eaten.

Recently I've been dreaming of cursing
old people, late at night, leaving scars
of oral surgery and needles.
They control the special light
in the center of the universe
that keeps us from dancing.
Emptiness.
They try to teach us things,
but if the question is:
what has replaced God
in my life, the answer is drinking
and being exceptionally social and not working.

I'm going to sit here
until I feel my soul,
early summer,
the whole neighborhood smells
like sperm.
"I feel sunburned with happiness!"
she cried. Did that mean she was
thinking of me?
I picked a flower for her every day
and kept it with my ammunition.

[I felt, at this point, that my brain was easing apart and two distinct but simultaneous consciousnesses were developing. I was in bed and my stomach ached because I ate too much at dinner. Then the candelabra excused itself into the night.]

HOMAGE TO ATTILA JOZSEF

My back hurts. On one side.
Also I feel that I am simply too large a creature,
that I am spindly. I have lost certain abilities.
I used to be a better driver.
Most of my pleasure comes from eating.
Eating fulfills more than hunger.
Carmina Burana touches me for personal reasons
related to performing it in high school; in other respects
I know it is worn and trite.
I am slowly wearing down my teeth.
I believe my dreams are real, with sincerity,
but am not sincere enough to move into them.
I have a physical condition which makes it impossible for me
    to fake interest.
I think everyone on TV looks like me.
I hold many conflicting beliefs. I take pride in this.
My anger is blunt and uncontrolled.
I am able to view nearly everything with a sense of wry
    detachment.
I am too ashamed to be unproductive.
I rely on humor to connect with people.

I try to view nearly every situation as humorous and detached.
People enjoy working with me.
In an office setting I am often described as "laid back."
I can type 67 words per minute.
I am at home,
in a chair,
available for work.
I am the right man for the job.

HOMAGE TO JOHN YAU

The most expert concerning the Godhead are the meek.
Meek little feet rain down on the ceiling.

Ceilings perform the most important function,
functioning as the dead-end of the room.

The room where we spoke has not awakened yet.
Yet even you are not sure if the pictures are listening.

Listen: do you hear that mysterious engine?
That engine burning and turning over our heads?

The head of every religion is allowed to witness this just once,
once they've drawn in their irresistible nets.

Now they're dropping nets off the roof, or is it rain?
If it's rain that falls, it's called squalls.

ABBOT

Other people's rules amuse me.
It's nice to be kissed without asking
for it. And dream of taking the exit off the freeway
to Buddhism. Anyone who breaks
stupid rules is a hero.
But what of a man
who willfully separates himself
from sex for the rest of his life?
There is something wrong
with him. He is like Yellowstone
National Park.
The bears.
Condors of eternal vigilance.
Only from a great height can he be forgiven.

HAPPY BIRTHDAY

Other people's love is perfect
in its imperfection, it leads the way
to the mountain meadow of flowers.
I have brought you this flower
from the high meadows of Colorado
with the full weight of blue summer
pressing down.
When I plucked it out the flower sighed.
Forget-me-not.
You lived in Firenze, and I was drunk.
I will always be drunk.

CLOUD WALK I

The blue and white sky
hangs behind the hemlocks
like a drape.

Tomorrow I go back
to the city.
I must fight to concentrate.

The sky is full of eyes.
Ferns are everywhere at once,
they are a blur of position and magnitude.

I lie on my back
among them thinking of sex,
of the positions and magnitude.

CLOUD WALK II

I was lying there
on the mossy ridge
thinking about gravity.

I climbed out to one of the farthest
points to try to drop off
into space,

to break the law and fall "up."
The punishment for that
is to constantly think of sex.

Then a friend approached me in the ferns.
"Stop talking to them," he shouted.
"They eat light!"

CLOUD WALK III

Back in the city
with everything.
I long to cross

the bridge to Toilet Island again,
Crossing back to money worries,
to their shame.

Then a woman's voice said
"There is no shame."
Her leg pressed against mine.

I must fight to concentrate.

THE MAN WHO TAUGHT MATT ROHRER HOW TO WRITE

We pulled off the main road to a side road
that passed by a small forest of gold trees.
Trees that were gold or gold-colored. Either way,
my inclination is to pursue magic
but the overweight man with the mustache
twisted the throttle and said *It would be a*
big mistake to ride through there, and I believed
him. But I would have walked right in.
The sun came up and the sky seemed far away,
though every day we're walking through the sky,
walking right in the middle of it.
The road was really steep.
I was only vaguely familiar with this guy
who had such self-control. He was taking me
to a party. He'd given me some poems
before at night. He appeared to me at night.

POEM FOR THEODORE

A party by the sea.
The night wet, grey, creaking
rhythmically. Rich, wide-open
smell of sea air. Rhythmic
people dancing, drinking
beer. I might as well be
here. Time isn't wasted
—all past moments spent
in whatever manner
lead equally to this moment,
when I drink this drink.
At the party I
even moved my arms when
I danced. This is a sign
I'm particularly
uninhibited.
The overweight man who
taught me to write at night
joins me. He drove me here.
Then I am struck
with a kind of blindness:
blindness of language.

I can't think of words whose
definitions become
ironic when I can't
speak them. Like, um, while the word
is in prison, I am not free.

EMU OF WONDER

They took me to see the Emu of Wonder
eat out of a sack.
They took me to see the Pronghorn pronking endlessly.
They took me to see the White Hart at night,
lit by headlights.
I hiked to the top of the falls to see the Coho surrender.
I heard the Pekinese suffering behind the dumpster.
You led me to the nest of the Golden Cockerel.

DOG BOY

ONE

Late at night in Oklahoma, a very small, an extremely small man ran across the road in front of my friend's car. He does not doubt this is real, though the rest of us do, and it doesn't bother him. He continues to paint portraits of astonishing trees each day and take long drives through the country at night. Nothing else can be learned about this mysterious incident.

TWO

On Scott Road, in Pittsburgh, which is a steep and winding city, full of good-natured people, just at the point where the road bottoms out beside a gnarled and ancient cemetery, a very small, an extremely small man ran across the road in front of my brother-in-law's car and scrambled into the tombstones. For the purposes of this story, I will refer to my brother-in-law as Matthew. Matthew had a friend in the car with him, and both of them saw this creature pass in front of them through the headlights. Matthew is the type to downplay this kind of thing, whether he dwells on it inwardly or not. Later, another friend of his who lives on Scott Road told Matthew he heard something outside one night and when he peered through the french doors he saw the same extremely small man leaping over the sandbox. How did he know it was the same one? I asked Matthew, and he shrugged and continued to strum an imaginary guitar, and Matthew's unconcern is the biggest mystery of them all.

DISAGREEABLE OBJECT (HOMAGE TO JOHN YAU)

Women who have been mounted by the devil
say his ding-a-ling is cold and rough.

Roughly half of the village reported seeing the disagreeable object
by the cliffs. Standing beside it, a colossal monopod, tall and thin.

A thin rain sweeps the green streets. The thin man
walks beside you, the fact of his single foot and leg disguised.

My disguise is to hang myself from the rafters
of the palace at 4 AM, a spine with no body.

The body is uneven and it is made of clay.
Ideas fly away like bees smoked out of the hive.

And the hive of ideas goes quiet. It shrinks
under its own weight. All that's left is crushed and rough.

A rough cold disagreeable object. Even the devil
wants nothing to do with it. He wants to look sexy.

DREAM OF A NEW PATRIOTISM

People tend to pair off, but not me.
I am alone in the forest.
The difference hangs before me like a mirror in air.
My friends have scattered,
and I cannot reach them
because the internal combustion engine
has been declared unpatriotic.

Then I awaken from my stupor.

The internal combustion engine is still our closest ally.
I'm in the park.
A man is painting a picture of the park
leaving out the litter and fence.
Little girls are calling my name
over the hills.

FOREST HAIKU

before you start—
do photographs make people happy
or sad

FOREST HAIKU

a good day,
bear tracks bypassing
an unsprung bear trap

FOREST HAIKU

rain over,
leaves drip on the tent.
her face is beautiful.

FOREST HAIKU

I look forward
to writing
different poems

SECOND POEM FOR THEODORE

Just pretend my writing is like somebody else's.
What things are important to you?
I am deeply concerned about your opinion of me.
To you I want to appear pleasant
& then invisible.
I want to be an interesting story
none of you really remembers.
Just a kind of nervous thing you have, really.
& then nothing.
Nothing.
Almost an eternity of nothing.
& then a terrible cataclysm.

SEVEN

is the magic number Heaven will topple
a tree on you crazy kid in the
wet street do you hear the streets
all keening that means you're
crazy Heaven will topple you
and drop its black minions
on you from the trees the
magic trees are laughing at
you look at yourself you're full
of magic holes.

HONE QUARRY

Walking up from the quarry
to Flagpole Knob, an old log
has fallen across the stream.
Each year I come here and stand
on one end. I cannot cross
it. I know it's a matter
of the mind, but my hair and
bones tremble, *they love The World.*

The Ranger—what's his job like?
As bad as mine? Didn't his father
tell him *never wear a*
uniform? Could one truly
fit you? This mountain road's bluish stones
seem, to me, the highest art.
They sing out beneath my feet.
What's it like to be their colleague?

Young couples, Mennonites, come
up through the trees to the water-
fall. They understand Time
differently. Things don't move
forward. They still wear bloomers.
They tear off the girls' bloomers.
We're all in agreement on this.
Then we move off, $^2/_7$ alive.

It rained in all the valleys
all night, we huddled and smoked
beneath a tarp. By morning
the world was flooded, rushing
water and broken hemlocks.
Locals came in trucks and laughed
at us trapped there with excuses.
This is how we're fooled by books.

If I accept suffering
will I pass as lightly as
these clouds? These messengers of
preexisting conditions?
After climbing to the bald
knob our world expands to fill
the valley. Those back in camp
are content, though, back in camp.

At night, lying on warm rocks
I hear whippoorwills answer
each other. Their timing is
sexual. I'm too stupid
to realize it's lonely, it's
an echo. I am in love
with the way I see the world.
But I am all alone there.

The day after rain tadpoles
spawn in a puddle in the
road. Their short war with the fact
of having been born begins.
We help a few to the creek.
By afternoon our hearts are
cold, we head to the river.
Cold river where we keep beer.

On top of a steep ridge there
is another world: mossy
stretches where we sleep beneath
the sky. Dozens of vultures
are circling something nearby.
We have all disappeared from
the world. Clouds pass or we pass
the clouds. We will never die.

Ritual of the drive in
the pick-up truck to the
woods. Shenandoah Valley
rises blue and grey early
morning. We pulled over to
sleep. Ground chill of quiet cows.
The invisible burden,
joy or sorrow, comes with you.

Dark night for the whippoorwill.
They all sound the same. Tonight
you are miles away. I hiked
to the bald summit but I
couldn't see you. You must be
dreaming under the streetlight.
How stirring. How saddening.
I can't believe animals.

Nature is underneath our
parting. I have come back to
report dead trees aren't really
dead. I could feel you thinking
about me while I washed in
the stream. It is good to be
alone in the trees. The whip-
poorwill will be your teacher.

Send the cry of the human
down the valley. You found the
Mossy Ridge. Daylight bats float
between trees there at the top
of a very small piece of
the world. We are ensorceled.
Everything fits together
without even knowing it.

Face of a dog in the tree.
If she were here, she'd see it.
Bats by daylight, everyone
thinks you lie. I believe in
nature, the wind that blows through
it is ample evidence.
I'm part of something bigger
which includes her, where she is.

Full moon on the cottonwoods.
That sounds like the first line of
a Chinese poem. My uncle
said it. Slovenians were
inspecting the surface of
the moon. The night was like a
palsied day, it offered us
only some of what we need.

You can't babysit the trees.
You can't tuck the rocks in at
night. You can't beckon the hawks
to your side. You can play a
game where you own all the land,
though, while you're here. You can own
all of the land. But you can't
teach the wild turkeys your name.

CATECHISM

Of my parents and origins I have little to say.

In church they actually told us
Catholicism was
"a big house full of cool, old stuff"

I spent my time sitting
in the darkened apse
imagining the actual house.

Your Dominican mind tricks don't work on me.

My knees suffered through Kumbaya.

Then there was the incident
of the professor who sneaked the holy water
out and poured it into the ocean.

He wrote a letter to the bishop
informing him that
all the world's water was holy now.

He was also a harborer of homosexuals.

I am still in the dark
imagining the actual house.

SUMMER SATURDAY MORNING

Mares' Tails in the air, they pose no threat.
Settle back into the grass
and the clear blue cushion of air.
There is nothing magical about the world,
or magic would have already won.
The world itself is soterial,
it is its own salvation.
And the sky is a soterial blue.
Concentrate carefully on the pathways of insects.

POEM FOR UNDERDOG

I have seen what others have only dreamed they've seen.
I have seen underdog in startling full-color
on a black and white TV.
I have seen the illicit mushroom activities on the moon.
I have seen the pandas in the darkened park.
The cashier at Sears who wore no bra;
the little brown and yellow cloud that hovered
over my grandparents' house; adults replaced
by Replicants in 1977; I have looked
into the mirror and seen two dark pools of humility.
Others have only dreamed they've looked into the mirror.

QUILT

If they take away the rotting pier

the rotting pier is the imagination.

But if they take away the rotting pier

they can't take away the quilt of lights

on the dark water, and the lights

on the dark water are the imagination.

The imagination will knit a sweater on the water.

THE GREAT SUBMARINE RACE

It's mad, but it just might work,
he said, and floridly signed his name
to The Great Submarine Race.

Submarines slumbered in his bloodstream
and submarines burbled in shallow slips.
The Flying Electrons bore the news
around the world on cold white draughts
and the news pierced the blue clouds.

A man in the square nudged his wife
and told her they were Mammary clouds.
Everyone's transmitter crackled.
Everyone's bloodstreams burbled faintly.

The wife loved the lumpy clouds.
The man's submarine slipped its mooring
and nosed her coral arches.
Simultaneously, all the world's submarines exhaled
and plunged deep into the shifting water,
with their little engines racing,
and when they met each other they battered one another's hearts.

SKI LIFT TO DEATH!

It was a basement with its own basement,
and in that basement were machines
and dusty weapons, the engines of the house;
where the floor gave way because of intense pressure
from below, and magma boiled up
through the wood-looking tiles;
where to leap to safety
broke my sister's foot;
where the animals that weren't as smart as we
were captured and admired;
where we watched in horror as the ski lift
lifted the men inexorably to death:

it was my favorite room in the house.

—

ANCIENT CHINESE WAR

It is bittersweet to read a dispatch
from an ancient Chinese war
and learn that change is illusory.
A heavy yoke pulls, a pleasant yoke
dragging me down.
This is my religion.
I worship on my back at night.
Even you, whom I revere,
you are only one blade of grass,
and a green light shows through.

MONGOLIAN DEATH WORM

ONE

They say in the dry flats of Mongolia, underneath the burning sun, burrows the Unnameable. Four feet long, or eight feet long, or two feet long, a pale, pudgy worm the mention of which brings death. It is not necessary to touch it to be killed by it; some say it spits poison, others that it emanates rings of death, like a radio. That no one has ever caught one should be no surprise; that no one who has seen one directly can be found should also produce in you yawns of recognition. I have lost interest already, in these few lines. I have been pausing for so long after each period, and nearly as long after each comma, there's no reason for you to still be here. There's nothing more to learn about the worm.

TWO

I did once try to find the Unnameable, years ago, but there is not much to say about it, and nothing for you to learn by reading any more. The plains were endless, and empty, the sun pressed down with all its might on the sand. My guides fell into torpor after seven days and refused to speak. I learned more from their horses, who were ribald and entertaining. One evening as the red sun burrowed into the crumbly hills the oldest guide shrieked and fell from his saddle, clutching his eyes. A great cacophony rose up from the horses, and a rare species of bright red bat rose up from the grass. But that is where the Definitive ends. After that came nightfall. Speculation.

THREE

The riders I encountered in the desert had fabulously gaudy tents. Their horses slept in them, or stayed awake bickering, but the riders would not sleep in the tents because they had no floors. When I asked what they were afraid of, they moved their fingers across their lips as if to signify a zipper, though I never saw a zipper in Mongolia. When, one bitter morning, we entered the tents to see why the horses had not joined us for breakfast and found them all dead, the riders quailed and zipped their lips. But I was unconvinced. Many mysterious things can occur in a tent full of horses.

STATUE OF A WHITE PIG BLEEDING FROM THE EYES

A man disappears into a hole in the street.
His shadow drifts away.
A terrible scream. The young priests
rush in to find men wearing colorful dresses,
with swallow-tailed sleeves,
kicking each other's hair.
This is novel. "They were doing it all
for a nickel."

■

Every breath I take splits Chinatown in half,
into cockamamie terror. You can
just read Euripides for the complete story.
"I am as guilty as any man who ever dreamed."
The man disappeared into the crypt
for a nickel—"the reek of dowagers
being gracious is also poison."

■

The young priest grapples with a shadowy man
over a foggy grate in the street.
Two men in dresses and make up kick
each other's hair in the shade
of the statue of the White Pig Bleeding From The Eyes.
The statue made them think they were somewhere else.
I travel through the night to visit my grandfather
but he's not where he should be.
A note on his door says "he was kidnapped for a nickel."

■

The terror of no clocks at all settles on me
in a dream. Then I wake up back in August
reek; I hate clocks again.
I put on a colorful dress and kick-start my hair.
My grandfather was down in Chinatown,
breaking up fights.
"There are mirrors there that make you think you are
    somewhere else."

WE NEVER SHOULD HAVE STOPPED AT PUSSY ISLAND

There is this desire to resurrect
the young grandfather
in his salt-stained fatigues,
but the fatigue of even pretending
to accompany him on the troopship
across the flat pale oceans
of the world sinks me
into the depths of the deep green couch.
There he was—riding into Manila
in the back of a jeep to restore communications,
surrounded by topless women
. running non-stop in circles around him.
Huge American planes lay fallen
into the very buildings
they had been attacking.
There was no stopping this thing.
In the photographs on the kitchen table
I look down the barrels of the ladies'
enormous dark areolas.
He never took off his boots there.

This heat presses me against the floor.
In Manila, long ago,
his sweat dissolved his clothes.
My wife is wearing his fatigues
tonight, and no bra; she is his size,
smooth and skinny legs.
They had to fuck up that whole island
to get it back and they were glad to have it.
The cows there were thinner than ours,
and hated both sides equally.
Boys were getting their bones ripped out
by bombs but it was also a safer time
to be alive—my grandfather's troopship
just swerved all over the sea and they were safe,
the enemy couldn't find them,
the only ones who knew where they were
were covered in scales, and the truth
could not be got from them.
And every move they made was a secret.
We do not know if they stopped
at any particular island.
The heat here turns into hot rain

as it did on his head
and the eviscerated boys
from Charlevoix blown back
into the trees. We do not know
why he did not call home, when he returned.
I do not even know what goes on
in the apartment upstairs.
We only know what the Army censors tell us.
Some boys simply disappeared,
never to wear ankle-high leather boots
with zippers, never to wake up
on a day that those were in fashion.

WINGED SNAKE FOUND ON A PATH

A long time ago, twelve hours from here
by car, on a small bit of acreage with a pond,
I was squatting in my shorts and contemplating
a poisoned, purple bean
when the grownups slapped it from my grasp.

It was hot in the air, in the furrows in the field.
It was cool on the black bottom of the pond,
and a chill rose from the deep
and settled under the trees.

I left the heat and circled the princely pond.
My head even then was too big,
and filled with trees.
And I almost did not see the winged snake
stretched across the path.
His long bright wings were battered and thin.
I knelt: someone had done him in.
And that was the last one I have seen.

LIKE A SAUSAGE

At the top of the park
I lean back on the bench
and survey the entire cosmos.
It is time to understand
my poetry.
The squirrels half-heartedly hide
from the young doberman pinscher
who hovers over the grass
in a blur.
Like a sausage.
Despite the squall
the world bursts into mirth.
I want the dog to bite the squirrel in half,
but my poetry does not.

MORNING GLORY ON THE ROOF

You have already noted the girlish beauty
of the Morning Glory,
the delicate lavender panties.
Looking around you,
as far as you can see,
plants are imprisoned.
Each morning Morning
Glories open upstairs,
out of sight.
Each night the concrete lies
like a hot compress on the dirt.
Thank you for your brief attention.

ACKNOWLEDGMENTS

Many of the poems in this book first appeared in literary magazines. I want to thank the editors for all of their work. "Winged Snake Found on a Path" appeared in *Denver Quarterly*. Thank you Bin Ramke. "Dog Boy," "Mongolian Death Worm," and "Morning Glory on the Roof" appeared in *The Iowa Review*. Thank you David Hamilton. "Emu of Wonder" and "The Great Submarine Race" appeared in *Ploughshares*. Thank you Heather McHugh. "Cloud Walk I," "Cloud Walk II," and "Cloud Walk III" appeared in/on the *Electronic Poetry Review*. Thank you D. A. Powell. "Dream of a New Patriotism" appeared in *Radical Society*. Thank you Joshua Beckman. "C" and "MK ULTRA" appeared in *Both*. Thank you Michael Brodeur. Parts of "Hone Quarry" appeared on *NowCulture.com* and in *NC2*. Thank you Ernie Hilbert. "Homage to John Yau" and "Disagreeable Object (Homage to John Yau)" appeared in *Columbia Journal*. Thank you Tiffany Noel Fung and Joel Whitney. "I Hail from the Bottom of the Sea, the Land of Eternal Darkness" and "Poem For Underdog" appeared in *The Canary*. Thank you Joshua Edwards. "Ancient Chinese War" appeared in/on *Slope*. Thank you Ethan Paquin. "Quilt" appeared in the *Contemporary Quilting Association Newsletter*. Thank you Linda Lunt and Katy Gollahon. "Homage to Attila Jozsef" and "Happy Birthday" appeared in *Crowd*. Thank you Brett Fletcher Lauer and Aimee Kelley. "Abbot" appeared in *Swink*. Thank you Lelila Strogov and David Hernandez. "The Adorable Little Boy" appeared in *Gulf Coast*. Thank you Michael Dumanis. "Like a Sausage," "Poem for Theodore," and "Second Poem for Theodore" appeared in *Court Green*. Thank you Tony Trigilio.

ABOUT THE AUTHOR

Matthew Rohrer is the author of *A Hummock in the Malookas*, which won the 1994 National Poetry Series and was published by W. W. Norton. *Satellite, Nice Hat. Thanks.* (with Joshua Beckman), and the audio CD *Adventures While Preaching the Gospel of Beauty* (with Joshua Beckman) were each published by Verse Press. He was born in Ann Arbor, grew up in Oklahoma, attended college in Ann Arbor and Dublin Ireland, and got an MFA in Iowa City. He lives in Brooklyn and is an editor for *Fence* magazine and Fence Books. His poems have appeared in many journals and anthologies, and have been translated into Slovenian, Finnish, and Portuguese.

DESIGNED AND COMPOSED AUGUST 2003 BY QUEMADURA

TEXT SET IN SCALA, DISPLAY SET IN AGENCY GOTHIC

PRINTED IN THE UNITED STATES BY THOMSON-SHORE, INC.